Does an Elephant Fit in Your Hand?

A Book About Animal Sizes

by Laura Purdie Salas

illustrated by Jeff Yesh

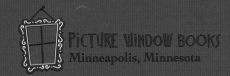

PICTURE WINDOW BOOKS
Minneapolis, Minnesota

Special thanks to our advisers for their expertise:

Zoological Society of San Diego
San Diego Zoo, San Diego, California

Susan Kesselring, M.A., Literacy Educator
Rosemount–Apple Valley–Eagan (Minnesota) School District

Editor: Christianne Jones
Designer: Nathan Gassman
Page Production: Melissa Kes
Creative Director: Keith Griffin
Editorial Director: Carol Jones
The illustrations in this book were created digitally.

Picture Window Books
5115 Excelsior Boulevard
Suite 232
Minneapolis, MN 55416
877-845-8392
www.picturewindowbooks.com

Printed in the United States of America.

Library of Congress Cataloging-in-Publication Data
Salas, Laura Purdie.
Does an elephant fit in your hand? : a book about animal sizes / by Laura Purdie Salas ;
illustrated by Jeff Yesh.
p. cm. — (Animals all around)
Includes bibliographical references.
ISBN-13: 978-1-4048-2235-1 (hardcover)
ISBN-10: 1-4048-2235-6 (hardcover)
1. Body size—Juvenile literature. I. Yesh, Jeff, 1971- ill. II. Title. III. Series.

QL799.3.S25 2007
590—dc22   2006003590

Editor's Note: There is often more than one species of each animal. The sizes described
in this book are a general overview of each animal, unless a specific species is noted.

Does an elephant fit in your hand?

No! A hummingbird fits in your hand.

The bee hummingbird is the world's smallest flying bird. It has a wingspan of only 1.3 inches (3.3 centimeters). Even with its wings spread, the hummingbird fits on a deck of cards.

Does an elephant have
huge wings?

No! An albatross has huge wings.

An albatross has the longest wingspan of any flying bird. Its wings spread 11 feet (3.4 meters) across. The albatross uses its long, skinny wings to capture wind. Then the bird can gracefully glide over the ocean without flapping its wings.

Does an elephant have a tiny, transparent body?

No! An infantfish has a tiny, transparent body.

The stout infantfish might be the smallest fish in the sea. This tiny fish could fit on top of the eraser at the end of your pencil. The stout infantfish has no coloring except in its eyes.

Does an elephant eat plankton ?

No! A shark eats plankton.

Whale sharks, the largest fish in the sea, can grow as long as two school buses. They eat tiny fish and plants called plankton. If a whale shark eats something rotten, it pushes its stomach out of its mouth. Then it empties the bad food back into the sea.

Does an elephant fit on a coin?

No! A gecko fits on a coin.

The dwarf gecko may be the world's smallest reptile. It measures about .75 inches (1.9 cm) long from its nose to the base of its tail. It's smaller than your thumb! The dwarf gecko lives in the Caribbean Islands.

Does an elephant have a heavy, dangerous tail?

No! A crocodile has a heavy, dangerous tail.

Saltwater crocodiles are the largest reptiles in the world. They can grow to 23 feet (7 m) long and weigh more than 2,200 pounds (990 kilograms). That's as heavy as nine refrigerators! A crocodile's large, flat tail can knock many animals off their feet.

Does an elephant grow inside other animals?

No! A wasp grows inside other animals.

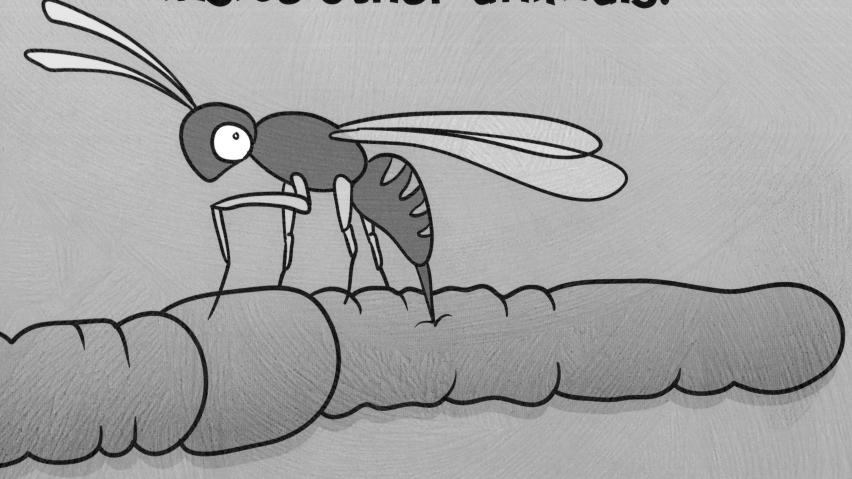

The parasitic wasp is one of the smallest insects in the world. It uses its stinger to lay eggs inside other animals. After the eggs hatch, babies spend part of their lives inside the host animal. More than 3,000 eggs can be laid in a single worm!

Does an elephant grow long horns?

No! A beetle grows long horns.

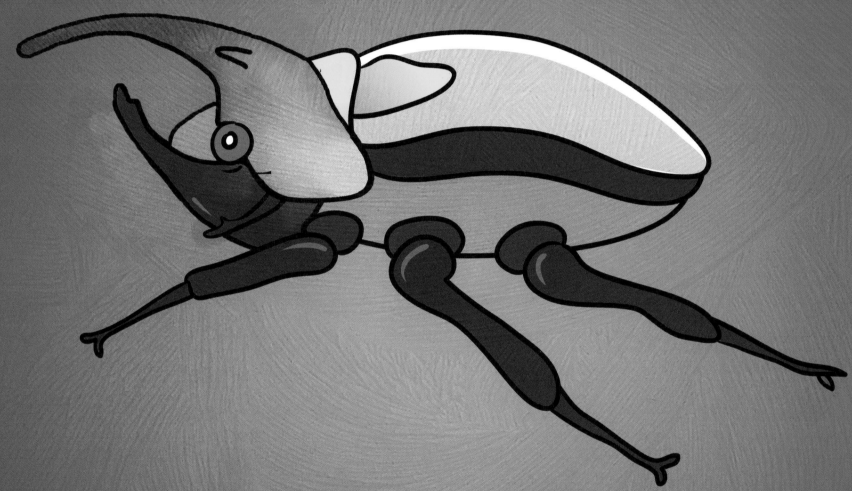

The male hercules beetle has large horns. These horns can be 2.5 to 4 inches (6 to 10 cm) long. They are used to fight other male beetles. Hercules beetles are one of the largest insects in the world.

Does an elephant weigh less than a grape?

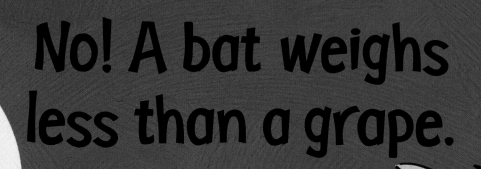

No! A bat weighs less than a grape.

The Kitti's hog-nosed bat, which lives in southeast Asia, is one of the smallest mammals in the world. It weighs less than 1 ounce (28 grams) and has a wingspan of less than 3 inches (7.6 cm). It is also called the bumblebee bat because of its tiny size.

Does an elephant weigh the same as a school bus?

Yes! An elephant weighs the same as a school bus.

African elephants are the largest land mammals in the world. They weigh about 14,000 pounds (6,300 kg). To keep up their energy, elephants eat more than 495 pounds (223 kg) of plants and leaves each day.

Different Animal Sizes

Some animals are small.

.... Bee hummingbirds have the shortest wingspan of any flying bird.

Stout infantfish are one of the smallest fish in the sea. ....

.... Dwarf geckos are one of the shortest reptiles.

Parasitic wasps are likely the shortest insect in the world. ....

...... Kitti's hog-nosed bats weigh less than any other known land mammal.

Some animals are large.

An albatross has the longest wingspan of any flying bird. ....

.... Whale sharks are the longest fish in the sea.

Saltwater crocodiles are the longest reptiles. ....

.... Hercules beetles are one of the largest insects in the world.

African elephants weigh more than any other land animal. ....

Glossary

capture—to catch and hold

host—an animal or plant that supports a parasite

parasitic—needing another animal for housing or food

plankton—small plants and animals that float in water

reptile—a cold-blooded animal with a backbone and scales

transparent—clear

wingspan—the length of a creature's outstretched wings measured from one tip to the other

To Learn More

At the Library

Bullard, Lisa. *Big and Small: An Animal Opposites Book.* Mankato, Minn.: Capstone Press, 2006.

Facklam, Margery. *The Big Bug Book.* Boston: Little, Brown and Company, 1992.

Wells, Robert E. *What's Smaller Than a Pygmy Shrew?* Morton Grove, Ill.: Albert Whitman & Company, 1995.

On the Web

FactHound offers a safe, fun way to find Internet sites related to this book. All of the sites on FactHound have been researched by our staff.

1. Visit *www.facthound.com*
2. Type in this special code for age-appropriate sites: 1404822356
3. Click on the FETCH IT button.

Your trusty FactHound will fetch the best sites for you!

Index

Look for all of the books in the Animals All Around series:

Do Bears Buzz? A Book About Animal Sounds
1-4048-0100-6
Do Bees Make Butter? A Book About Things Animals Make
1-4048-0288-6
Do Cows Eat Cake? A Book About What Animals Eat
1-4048-0101-4
Do Crocodiles Dance? A Book About Animal Habits
1-4048-2230-5
Do Dogs Make Dessert? A Book About How Animals Help Humans
1-4048-0289-4
Do Ducks Live in the Desert? A Book About Where Animals Live
1-4048-0290-8
Do Frogs Have Fur? A Book About Animal Coats and Coverings
1-4048-0292-4
Do Goldfish Gallop? A Book About Animal Movement
1-4048-0105-7
Do Lobsters Leap Waterfalls? A Book About Animal Migration
1-4048-2234-8
Do Parrots Have Pillows? A Book About Where Animals Sleep
1-4048-0104-9
Do Pelicans Sip Nectar? A Book About How Animals Eat
1-4048-2233-X
Do Penguins Have Puppies? A Book About Animal Babies
1-4048-0102-2
Do Polar Bears Snooze in Hollow trees? A Book About Animal Hibernation
1-4048-2231-3
Do Salamanders Spit? A Book About How Animals Protect Themselves
1-4048-0291-6
Do Squirrels Swarm? A Book About Animal Groups
1-4048-0287-8
Do Turtles Sleep in Treetops? A Book About Animal Homes
1-4048-2232-1
Do Whales Have Wings? A Book About Animal Bodies
1-4048-0103-0
Does an Elephant Fit in Your Hand? A Book About Animal Sizes
1-4048-2235-6